IMAGES
of America

FORT ORD

IMAGES
of America

FORT ORD

Harold E. Raugh, Jr.

ARCADIA

Published by Arcadia Publishing
Charleston SC, Chicago IL, Portsmouth NH, San Francisco CA

Printed in the United States of America

Library of Congress Catalog Card Number: 2003115616

For all general information contact Arcadia Publishing at:
Telephone 843-853-2070
Fax 843-853-0044
E-Mail sales@arcadiapublishing.com
For customer service and orders:
Toll-Free 1-888-313-2665

Visit us on the Internet at www.arcadiapublishing.com

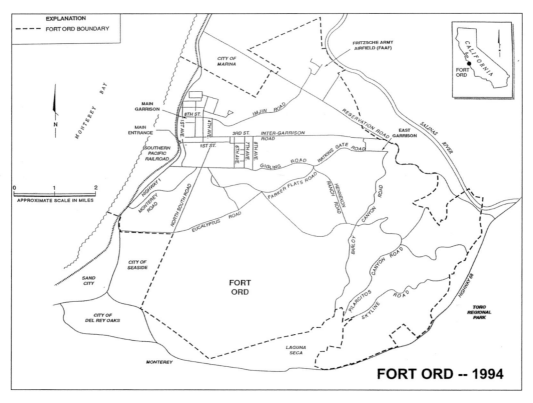

CONTENTS

Acknowledgments   6

Introduction   7

1.   1917–1940: From Camp Gigling to Camp Ord   9

2.   1940–1945: Ford Ord and the 7th Infantry Division   31

3.   1946–1976: The Cold War and the Vietnam Eras   81

4.   1974–1994: The Volunteer Army and Low-Intensity Conflict   107

5.   Post-1994: From Swords to Plowshares   121

ACKNOWLEDGMENTS

I am grateful to have had the opportunity to serve two tours of duty as an Infantryman in the 7th Infantry Division (Light) at Fort Ord, California. I hope the publication of this pictorial history of Fort Ord will help preserve the history and heritage of a fine military installation and of the memory of superb soldiers who served there.

Many of the photographs in this book are from the Historical Documents Collection (Archives) of the Defense Language Institute Foreign Language Center and Presidio of Monterey (DLIFLC & POM), a post that for many years served as a tenant of Fort Ord. I appreciatively acknowledge permission to reproduce these photographs here. Many of these photographs were donated to the DLIFLC & POM Archives by, among others, the following: Pastor Dan Appel, whose father, Sgt. Melvin C. Appel, served at Fort Ord during World War II; Sgt. Maj. Bob Britton, U.S. Army (Ret.); Col. Clarence N. Bowen, U.S. Air Force (Ret.), who trained at Camp Ord in the 1930s while an officer in the 361st Infantry Regiment, 91st Infantry Division; Jack W. Peters, who served in the 10th Field Artillery, 3rd Division, at Camp Ord, in 1940, and Maj. Gen. and Mrs. Robert G. Fergusson, U.S. Army (Ret). General Fergusson commanded the U.S. Army Training Center, Infantry, and Fort Ord, 1965–1967. Many of the other photographs presented here were taken by official U.S. Army photographers.

Proceeds from the sale of this book will be donated to the Fort Ord Alumni Association to assist in awarding scholarships to students at the California State University-Monterey Bay and to help further preserve the history and heritage of Fort Ord.

——Harold E. Raugh, Jr.
Lieutenant Colonel, U.S. Army (Ret.)

INTRODUCTION

The U.S. Army installation best known as Fort Ord, California, from its establishment in 1917 during World War I to its closure in 1994 after the end of the Cold War, made a significant contribution to the defense of the United States.

On August 4, 1917, the U.S. War Department purchased 15,609.5 acres of land from the David Jacks Corporation to be used as a training area and firing range for the infantry, cavalry, and field artillery units stationed at the Presidio of Monterey. This included one large parcel of 15,409.5 acres and a smaller area of 200 acres next to Jacks' railroad siding. This acquisition, today known as the East Garrison area, was then called Gigling Reservation, named after a German immigrant family that had lived on the land.

Army units at the Presidio of Monterey organized several Civilian Conservation Corps (CCC) camps in the area in 1933, including one on Gigling Reservation. The training area was also used by units from the Presidio of San Francisco, the California Army National Guard, the Citizens Military Training Corps, and the Reserve Officer Training Corps. These units frequently bivouacked in a section of Gigling Reservation called Camp Huffman, located west of Merrillis Hill.

Also in 1933, the Army renamed Gigling Reservation "Camp Ord" after Maj. Gen. E.O.C. Ord (1818–1883), a prominent Civil War commander who had first arrived in Monterey in January 1847 as a lieutenant in Company F, 3rd Artillery. In 1938, the Army built permanent buildings and facilities on the bluffs overlooking Salinas that later became known as East Garrison.

The Army began to prepare for war in 1939 by selecting sites for training a proposed conscript army. Monterey Bay seemed to be vulnerable to an enemy invasion, and in early 1940, the Fourth Army conducted in the Monterey Bay area the first major joint Army-Navy operation on the West Coast since World War I.

In 1940, the Army bought an additional 3,777 acres of land located between Marina and the existing Camp Ord. Later that same year, an additional 2,000 acres east of Highway 1 and north of Seaside to the Gigling railroad spurs were purchased. Also in 1940, residents of the Salinas and Monterey areas bought a 276.4-acre parcel of land south of Marina and west of the railroad line and donated it to the Army. The latter became the beach rifle ranges.

Construction began on the new installation in 1940. The portion of the garrison located near the coast was temporarily named Camp Clayton, and another part of the camp was named Camp Pacific. On August 15, 1940, Camps Ord, Huffman, Clayton, and Pacific were combined and redesignated Fort Ord, which became a permanent Army installation.

Fort Ord was built in 1940–1941 at a cost of $12 million, the largest single construction project ever undertaken in the Monterey Bay area. Within months, the infrastructure of a medium-sized town, with roads and railroad sidings, water and sewer lines, power and telephone lines, and hundreds of temporary wooden "mobilization buildings," was completed. By January 1942, Fort Ord consisted of 28,514 acres.

The 7th Infantry Division (7ID), which had been initially constituted on December 6, 1917 at Camp Wheeler, Georgia, participated in combat operations in Europe in World War I, and was inactivated on September 22, 1921 at Camp Meade, Maryland. For service in World War II, the 7ID was reactivated on July 1, 1940 at Camp Ord, California, under the command of Maj. Gen. (later Gen.) Joseph W. Stilwell (1883–1946). After extensive training, the 7ID deployed to Alaska in January 1943 for the recapture of the Aleutians. The 7ID emerged from World War II as a battle-hardened unit, having fought in four Pacific Theater campaigns and having lost 1,116 soldiers killed in action and almost 6,000 wounded in action.

In 1942, the 2nd Filipino Infantry Regiment was activated at Fort Ord. Many additional Army units trained at Fort Ord from 1942 to 1944, including the 3rd, 27th, 35th, and 43rd Infantry Divisions. German and Italian prisoners of war were also held at Fort Ord, which became a replacement center for individual infantrymen in 1944. The peak strength of Fort Ord during World War II was over 50,000 soldiers.

After the end of World War II in 1945, Fort Ord became a major demobilization center. The post was designated the 4th Replacement Training Center in 1947. In 1949, the center was redesignated the 4th Infantry Division and, in 1950, the 6th Infantry Division. (These were training divisions, not combat divisions like the 7th Infantry Division.) In 1956, the 5th Infantry Division redeployed from Germany and operated the training center. The Army stopped designating training centers as infantry divisions in 1957, when the post was redesignated the U.S. Army Training Center, Infantry, Fort Ord, California.

Fort Ord was a basic training center during the Vietnam War. In December 1970, Fort Ord was one of four Army posts selected to participate in Project VOLAR (Voluntary Army), which was launched in January 1971 with the goal of determining the effectiveness of certain resource expenditures in an effort to achieve a "zero draft" by July 1, 1973. Barracks were remodeled, KP duty was eliminated, and a new post exchange was built in 1970. In 1971, the Army at Fort Ord began to experiment with new methods of instruction called EVATP (Experimental Volunteer Army Training Program) that provided for "hands-on" training. VOLAR was phased out at the end of fiscal year 1972 when the Army concentrated on building the Modern Volunteer Army (MVA). In 1972, Fort Ord ceded 550 acres on its southeast boundary to Seaside.

After World War II service, the 7ID performed occupation duty in Korea (1945–1948) and Japan (1948–1950). The Division, given the nickname the "Bayonet Division," fought throughout the 1950–1953 Korean War and distinguished itself at the Inchon landings and at the Chosin Reservoir. The 7ID returned to the United States in 1971after 28 years overseas. The Division was inactivated on April 2, 1971 at Fort Lewis, Washington, and reactivated on October 21, 1974 at Fort Ord. Basic training ended at Fort Ord in 1976.

In 1983, as a result of the military experience on Grenada and in other operations, the Army reassessed the changing nature of warfare and the force structures of its units. Standard infantry divisions were to be replaced by new light infantry divisions of about 10,000 men that were rapidly deployable. The 7ID was designated to be the first of four light infantry divisions and began its transition to light infantry division structure in 1984. The 7ID grew from a division of two infantry brigades with a National Guard round-out brigade to a full division of three infantry brigades with a combat aviation brigade. The 7ID was redesignated the 7th Infantry Division (Light) on October 1, 1985 and was deployable three times faster than any infantry division then existing. This concept was put to the test as the 7ID(L) deployed to Panama in December 1989 and participated in Operation Just Cause. Fort Ord later served as a major mobilization center for Operations Desert Shield and Desert Storm in 1990–1991.

In 1991, with the end of the Cold War, the Presidential Base Realignment and Closure Committee (BRAC) included Fort Ord in its list of 35 military facilities slated for closure. In 1993, the 1st Brigade, 7ID(L) moved to Fort Lewis, and the remainder of the 7ID(L) inactivated officially on June 16, 1994 at Fort Lewis. Fort Ord closed on September 30, 1994. The Army retained 795 acres of the former Fort Ord and renamed it the Ord Military Community, a sub-component of the Presidio of Monterey.

One

1917–1940

FROM CAMP GIGLING TO CAMP ORD

This new U.S. Army recruit smiles broadly as his photograph is taken outside his tent at Camp Ord, California, on August 15, 1940. He is armed with the Model 1903 Springfield service rifle, which was manufactured from 1903 to 1945. It was the primary U.S. combat rifle until replaced by the M1 Garand in 1936, although it continued to be used through World War II.

The War Department initially purchased 15,609.5 acres of land from the David Jacks Corporation on August 4, 1917 to use as training and range areas for units assigned to the Presidio of Monterey. Other units used the area for summer maneuvers. This area, near what is today known as East Garrison, was originally called the Gigling Reservation, or Camp Gigling, after the German family that originally homesteaded the area. From 1917 until 1938, the area contained only a well, a caretaker's house, and a few bivouac sites. East Garrison and the Gigling railroad spur on California State Highway 1 were originally connected by a rough dirt road. This directional sign to Camp Gigling is spelled inaccurately.

To the amazement of onlooking soldiers, an Army blimp flies over the Parker Flats area of the Gigling Reservation during training in 1932.

In 1933, Camp Gigling was renamed Camp Ord, after Maj. Gen. E.O.C. Ord , a prominent Civil War commander. A Civilian Conservation Corps (CCC) camp was established at Camp Ord, as noted on this entrance sign and archway to Camp Ord in a photo taken on July 9, 1937.

These soldiers are shown around their .37 mm pack howitzer at Camp Ord in 1938.

Prior to World War II, many cavalry and field artillery units depended upon horses for their means of transportation and to tow their artillery. In this c. 1938 photograph are a number of the horses of the 11th Cavalry Regiment, then stationed at the Presidio of Monterey, while training at Camp Ord.

Beware of Army dog! Many Army units, notably cavalry and artillery units with horses, and especially in the field, had animal mascots in the years prior to World War II. In this 1940 Camp Ord photograph, a canine mascot of the 10th Field Artillery, 3rd Infantry Division, poses behind a unit Browning M2 .50 caliber machine gun. The M2 version of this machine gun, here mounted on an M3 tripod, has a maximum effective range of 2,000 meters.

Soldiers of the 361st Infantry Regiment, Organized Reserve Corps, conduct rifle marksmanship training during their annual summer training period at Camp Ord, July 17, 1937.

Members of the 361st Infantry Regiment conduct live-fire training on the .81 mm mortar, July 17, 1937, at Camp Ord. These mortars used their curved-projectory fire to kill enemy soldiers in the open or in light defensive positions.

2nd Lt. (later Col., U.S. Air Force) Clarence N. Bowen, 361st Infantry Regiment, fires the Browning M1917A1 .30 caliber water-cooled machine gun on a range at Camp Ord on July 17, 1937. This was the standard machine gun of U.S. forces in World War I and was used extensively in World War II.

2ND BN. 15TH INF. CAMP ORD. CAL.

This photograph shows the bell tent bivouac site of the 2nd Battalion, 15th Infantry, at Camp Ord in 1940.

Pictured here are the gun park (foreground) and bivouac site (background) of the 10th Field Artillery, Camp Ord, in 1940. A number of the trucks are prepared to tow their artillery pieces, which seem to be the M116 .75 mm pack howitzer with pneumatic tires.

As shown in this 1940 photograph, Camp Ord at the time consisted only of tents when units were training and a few wooden buildings used for headquarters and supply room purposes.

This is another view of the "tent city" at Camp Ord c. 1940. These tents were occupied at the time by soldiers of the 30th Infantry Regiment, who traveled from the Presidio of San Francisco each summer to train at Camp Ord.

When in training, four soldiers normally lived in the commonly used bell tents. This 1940 Camp Ord photograph shows the interior of the bell tent with the four artillery soldiers who lived there and their cots, footlockers, and other equipment. The stove in the center of the tent was used for heating purposes, as it gets quite chilly at night in the Camp Ord area.

This 1939 Camp Ord photograph reveals the cement platforms on which the bell tents were erected.

The seasonal winter rains at Camp Ord could turn dusty roads into veritable quagmires overnight. In this 1940 photograph, a tracked bulldozer-type vehicle is extricating a truck from the mud.

The torrential run-off from the heavy winter rains at Camp Ord in 1940 frequently washed away tents and soaked the soldiers' equipment, thus delaying training.

It's chow time in the field at Camp Ord in this 1940 photograph. At this time, each infantry company or artillery battery had its own cooks and mess hall facilities. Here, a cook prepares what looks like hamburger patties on the mobile field cooking range.

Soldiers of B Battery, 10th Field Artillery, begin crew drill training on their .75 mm howitzers at Camp Ord in 1940.

This large circus-type tent was erected at Camp Ord in 1940 to serve as a theater in which to show motion pictures to soldiers at night and other times when they were not training. Movies and other forms of entertainment helped raise soldier morale.

Much of the artillery in the U.S. Army prior to World War II, as noted previously, was still horse drawn. This photograph shows horse-drawn artillery of the 76th Field Artillery passing in review during Army Day activities at Camp Ord in 1940.

Soldiers conduct semaphore training as members of B Battery, 10th Field Artillery, conduct crew drill in the background. In the center of this 1940 photograph is Corp. Jack W. Peters.

The Browning M1917A1 .30 caliber water-cooled machine gun, used extensively in World War II, is shown here being fired by infantrymen at Camp Ord in 1940.

Soldiers of E Company, 4th Regiment, 3rd Infantry Division pass in review during Army Day activities at the Parker Flats area of Camp Ord on April 6, 1940. The following series of

A U.S. light tank (probably the M2A2 model), with the name "Cyclone" painted on the turret, demonstrates its mobility and maneuverability during Army Day activities.

photographs were all taken at that event 1940.

11th Cav. passing in review. Army Day. Camp Ord. 1940 177

The horse-mounted 11th Cavalry Regiment, then stationed at the nearby Presidio of Monterey, passes in review.

Artillery pieces, seemingly .75 mm howitzers, are towed by their truck prime movers as this field artillery battery passes in review.

During Army Day activities, soldiers from H Battery, 10th Field Artillery, demonstrate their speed and proficiency in getting their guns into action.

A live firing exercise with trench mortars is demonstrated during the April 6, 1940 Army Day activities.

Large .155 mm howitzers are fired at Camp Ord during Army Day activities.

This photograph shows the tent encampment of the 11th Cavalry Regiment at Camp Ord during the late 1930s. The wooden buildings served as mess halls (dining facilities) for the

Telephone Display Camp Ord Calif. Army Day. April 6, 1940. 154.

A tactical field telephone is on display in this photograph from Army Day activities at Camp Ord, April 6, 1940.

soldiers. The white object hanging from the tripod in the left center of the photograph is a Lister bag, containing potable water for drinking.

This group of soldiers, with their canine mascot, poses while standing in the chow line at Camp Ord, c. 1940. Note the mess kits and canteen cups held by the soldiers; these were pieces of Army equipment that did not change for decades.

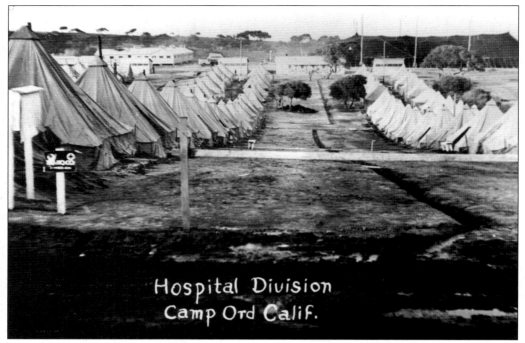

Hospital Division
Camp Ord Calif.

The 3rd Medical Battalion, 3rd Infantry Division, contained the unit's medical facilities. In the absence of permanent buildings, bell tents held all medical treatment facilities and housed the unit's soldiers while training in the Camp Ord area, 1940.

POST EXCHANGE NO.2. CAMP ORD.
NEAR SALINAS, CALIF. 101.

This building housed the Post Exchange (PX) at Camp Ord in January 1940. The two ice cream trucks at the left of this photograph making their delivery to the PX suggest that ice cream was in high demand by training soldiers!

This 1940 aerial photograph shows Camp Ord perched on the bluffs (to the left and bottom of the photograph) overlooking the fertile Salinas River Valley. The two large rectangular features consist of tents in bivouac.

Camp Ord was named after Maj. Gen. E.O.C. Ord. Ord, born in 1818, was a lieutenant in Company F, 3rd Artillery Regiment, and among the first U.S. Army troops to land in Monterey on January 26, 1847 and to participate in the construction of Fort Mervine. He later distinguished himself in the Civil War, most significantly as commander in one of the North's earliest victories at Dranesville, Virginia. He was later a prominent participant in the siege of Vicksburg and was a senior commander in the final drive against Richmond and Petersburg that culminated in Appomattox. After the Civil War, Ord commanded the departments of Arkansas, California, Texas, and the Platte. In 1881, he retired from the Army and died two years later.

Two
1940–1945
FORT ORD AND THE
7TH INFANTRY DIVISION

The first real work at Camp Ord began in 1938 when a large area, about a mile east of the Gigling railroad spur, was cleared by Presidio of Monterey soldiers and Work Progress Administration (WPA) laborers. In 1940, additional land, between Marina and the existing Camp Ord, and north of Seaside to the Gigling railroad spurs, was acquired by the Army. The area located closest to the coast was initially called Camp Clayton. Construction of buildings at Camp Clayton, such as the one depicted in this photograph, began in 1940.

The 7th Division was reactivated on July 1, 1940, under the command of Brig. Gen. Joseph W. Stilwell (shown here as a lieutenant general *c.* 1942, when Stilwell was commanding the China-Burma-India Theater). On July 10, 1940, Stilwell assumed command of the Camp Ord Military Reservation and the Presidio of Monterey.

On August 15, 1940, Camp Clayton, Camp Ord (East Garrison), Camp Huffman (a small training area near the Parker Flats/Eucalyptus Road area), and Camp Pacific (an engineer compound south of First Street and east of North-South Road) were combined and officially renamed Fort Ord. This photograph shows concrete foundations for buildings at Fort Ord being poured under the supervision of foreman Jimmy Norman (right).

The government laundry facility was also built on Fort Ord in 1940.

This row of warehouses was built along Fourth Avenue on Fort Ord c. 1940. (A few of these warehouses, probably the five on the right of the photograph, were torn down in 2003; the other warehouses remain standing.)

Thousands of these temporary "mobilization buildings," each designed to serve as a platoon barracks, were constructed at Fort Ord in 1940 and 1941. These buildings were constructed according to a standard Quartermaster Corps plan and were identical to other buildings constructed at continental U.S. military installations at the beginning of World War II. These buildings were designed to last only long enough to be used through the end of World War II and were never intended for permanent occupation.

)16-46-F-IE)(9-14-40-10:30A)(12-1340) CAMP CLAYTON

This aerial photograph of the original Camp Clayton section of Fort Ord was taken by the 1st Photographic Section, Flight E., U.S. Army Air Corps, Moffett Field, California, on September 14, 1940. In this photograph, taken facing east with Highway 1 in the foreground, very few buildings have been constructed. The 7th Infantry Division soldiers remained encamped mainly in bell tents, seen in bivouac in the center of the photograph.

O18-46-F-IE)(9-14-40-10:35A)(12-1360) CAMP CLAYTON

Also taken on September 14, 1940, this aerial photograph depicts the area to the south of that in the previous photograph. A few of the original mobilization buildings can be seen in various stages of construction in the center of this photograph.

029-46B-82 (11-20-40-12:55P)(12-1000) CAMP CLAYTON , CALIF.

This aerial photograph of the northernmost section of the Fort Ord main cantonment area was taken by the 82nd Observation Squadron, U.S. Army Air Corps, Moffett Field, California, on November 20, 1940. The front row shows mobilization buildings in stages of construction from start to finish. The large building (with two wings) in the center left of this photograph is the Fort Ord Post Headquarters.

The rapid transformation of the Fort Ord main garrison area from a tent city to a cantonment with hundreds of buildings can be seen in this aerial photograph taken on November 20, 1940. Monterey Bay can be seen at the top of this photograph, taken facing west.

026-46B-82)(11-20-40-12:51P)(12-1000) CAMP CLAYTON, CALIF.

This aerial photograph of the Fort Ord main garrison area was taken facing northwest on November 20, 1940.

The Fort Ord military hospital is shown under construction in the foreground of this November 20, 1940 photograph, taken facing south. A glimpse of Monterey Bay is visible in the top right corner.

046-46B-82)(1-11-41-10:10 A)(2-1200) CAMP CLAYTON, CALIF

The Fort Ord military hospital is basically completed in this January 11, 1941 aerial photograph, taken facing north by the 82nd Observation Squadron, U.S. Army Air Corps, Moffett Field, California. Covered walkways connecting the various hospital buildings can be seen under construction.

5-46B-82)(1-11-41- 10:10A)(12 - 1200) CAMP CLAYTON. CALIF.

This January 11, 1941 photograph, taken facing north (with the town of Marina in the background), depicts the northernmost section of the Fort Ord main garrison area. The Fort Ord Post Headquarters is the building in the center touching the right-hand margin of the photograph. The large building, located slightly to the left of the Post Headquarters building, was Movie Theater No. 3.

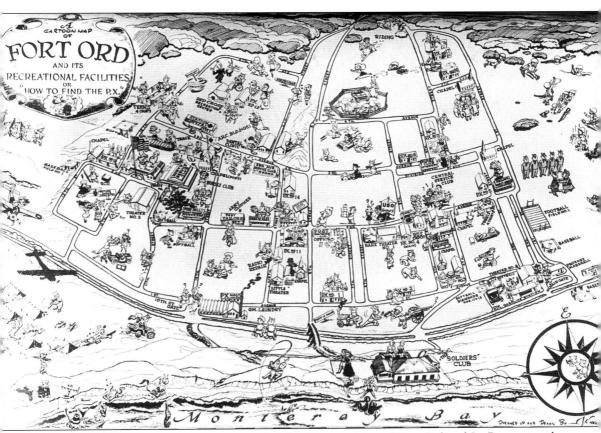

This World War II–era caricature is entitled, "A Cartoon Map of Fort Ord and Its Recreational Facilities, or 'How to find the P.X.'" This map is facing east, with Monterey Bay in the foreground.

This aerial view shows Fort Ord, *c.* 1943, facing Monterey Bay in the west. The main street running from the upper left-hand corner to the lower right-hand corner of this photograph is First Street, which was the southernmost boundary of Fort Ord's main garrison area during World War II.

This is the Fort Ord physical training area, *c.* 1943, directly south of First Street.

Fort Ord soldiers develop teamwork and physical fitness during these *c.* 1943 log-drill physical training exercises.

The main garrison of Fort Ord was completed in 1941 at a cost of about $12 million, making it the largest single construction project ever undertaken in the Monterey Bay area. This is what part of it looked like *c.* 1943.

Post Chapel and Red Cross Bldg. - Fort Ord

The main Post Chapel (at left in this *c.* 1943 photograph) was located next to the American Red Cross Headquarters on Tenth Street near its intersection with Third Avenue.

Station Hospital - Fort Ord

The headquarters building of the Fort Ord Station Hospital, as shown in this *c.* 1943 photograph, was located on Third Avenue.

Soldiers pass in review during a ceremony at the Fort Ord main Parade Field, *c.* 1943.

These soldiers at a bivouac site have used their shelter halves to construct two-man tents at Fort Ord during World War II.

Soldiers fire the M1919A4 .30 caliber air-cooled machine gun at Fort Ord during World War II. The M1919A4 was not able to sustain the same rate of fire or accuracy as the M1917A1 .30 caliber water-cooled machine gun, but the former (with tripod) weighed only 41 pounds and the latter (with tripod) weighed 93 pounds.

In this photograph, Col. F.C. Sibert, commanding officer of the 32nd Infantry, one of the three infantry regiments (along with the 17th and 53rd Infantry Regiments) of the 7th Infantry Division in 1941, conducts a full field gear layout inspection of his soldiers at Fort Ord on March 12, 1941.

Soldiers of the 32nd Infantry Regiment cross an improvised floating bridge during training at Fort Ord, March 1941.

Infantry soldiers prepare to build a floating mattress bridge during training at Fort Ord in March 1941.

Many units (including the 7th, 35th, 3rd, 27th, and 43rd Divisions) conducted amphibious and other training at Fort Ord prior to deployment to participate in combat operations in the Pacific Theater and elsewhere. One of these units was the 53rd Infantry Regiment of the 7th Infantry Division. In this 1941 Fort Ord photograph, a tower is draped with a cargo net/rope ladder, and the soldiers are climbing it to simulate climbing from a landing craft into a ship (or vice versa) or up a wharf at an important objective.

These 53rd Infantry Regiment soldiers are training in climbing from an actual wharf (the Monterey Municipal Wharf) down to boats, in which they will conduct an amphibious beach landing, July 1941.

Soldiers of the 53rd Infantry Regiment are conducting boat landing maneuvers at Del Monte Beach on Monterey Bay, July 1941.

The stalwart soldiers standing in front of their Fort Ord barracks in this May 5, 1941 photograph were the original cadre members of the 31st Field Artillery. The 31st Field Artillery was a .155 mm truck-drawn howitzer regiment.

The sun sets over Fort Ord, with the Monterey Peninsula edging the horizon in the background. This photograph was taken by Corp. Chester Burns of the Fort Ord Camera Club on February 18, 1941.

Truck-drawn artillery, believed to be from the 147th Field Artillery, Fort Ord, conducts vehicular convoy training on the roads passing through majestic redwood forests north of Santa Cruz in 1941.

During the same 1941 training exercise, two vehicles of the 147th Field Artillery—a Willy's jeep on the left and an M2 wheeled combat car on the right—pause under the redwoods north of Santa Cruz.

During a *c.* 1941 training exercise at Fort Ord, a captain communicates on a field radio.

A mortar crew prepares for action during this *c.* 1941 training exercise at Fort Ord.

Soldiers of the 17th Infantry conduct training on the .37 mm anti-tank gun at Fort Ord in 1941.

The unit field kitchen is established during a field training exercise at Fort Ord, *c.* 1941.

Soldiers move through the chow line and get their mess kits filled during a *c.* 1941 Fort Ord field exercise.

A soldier inflates his air mattress while in a bivouac site during a Fort Ord field training exercise, *c.* 1941.

The bazooka, developed by an American, was a short-range weapon that gave the infantryman the means of destroying armored vehicles and fortified positions. It consisted of a lightweight metal tube from which rockets were launched and generally had a crew of two men, a gunner and a loader. It was used extensively during World War II. In this photograph, Fort Ord soldiers fire their bazookas at a training range during World War II.

These two camouflaged M2 wheeled combat cars drive north on Second Avenue on Fort Ord in 1941. The large building in the left background was Movie Theater No. 1, and the smaller building on the right was the local civilian bank branch.

Technology did not replace all means of transportation and modes of combat, as shown in this September 25, 1941 photograph showing a quartermaster pack train exercise at Fort Ord.

Under General Stilwell's orders, Fort Ord soldiers made and used Molotov cocktails. A Molotov cocktail is a simple, hand-held firebomb, an incendiary weapon that is effective against personnel, vehicles, and buildings. In this August 1, 1941 photograph, a Fort Ord sergeant holds the Molotov cocktail in his right hand and prepares to pull the flare igniter with his left hand.

This August 1, 1941 photograph depicts the Molotov cocktail as the flare igniter begins to burn.

This Fort Ord infantry officer prepares to throw the Molotov cocktail in the same manner that he would throw a hand grenade. Infantrymen, especially in combat, need to be versatile fighters familiar with many types of unconventional and other weapons.

Pvt. Lonny Wilson, wearing a Brodie-type helmet and OD (olive drab) wool shirt, is pictured while training at Fort Ord, c. 1940. Even though his face was encrusted with mud, Wilson was smiling and reportedly said, "We don't mind a little dirt."

Hollywood movie stars, radio personalities, and comedians frequently visited Fort Ord during World War II to give performances and help raise soldier morale. Jack Benny and his real-life wife, Mary Livingstone, were leading stars who visited Fort Ord c. 1941.

George Burns and Gracie Allen were surrounded by 32nd Infantry Regiment and other soldiers when they visited Fort Ord *c.* 1941. The ribbon worn by George Burns states, "Motion Picture Production Defense Committee of Hollywood."

Movie star Claudette Colbert (right, in back of jeep) visited 7th Infantry Division soldiers at Fort Ord *c.* 1941.

The Ritz Brothers, a comedic group that appeared in many movies in the late 1930s and early 1940s, visited Fort Ord c. 1941.

Eddie "Rochester" Anderson, the brash butler from Jack Benny's comedy show, also visited Fort Ord c. 1941.

Four or five motion pictures were also filmed entirely or in part at Fort Ord. "Steel Cavalry" was the working title of the movie filmed at Fort Ord in 1941 and released in 1942 as *The Bugle Sounds*. Wallace Beery (left in tank turret) played an old cavalry sergeant who was discharged for insubordination but won reinstatement back into the Army. This movie, directed by S.E. Simon, also starred Lewis Stone and Marjorie Main.

This all-female singing and dancing troupe entertained Fort Ord soldiers c. 1941. The standing trumpeter wears the 3rd Infantry Division patch. The 3rd Infantry Division mobilized and trained at Fort Ord in 1941 and 1942.

Music frequently helped raise soldiers' spirits, and this quartet presented special music at the 1st Medical Regiment's church service on December 13, 1942 at Fort Ord. The soldier-musicians are, from left to right, Pvt. Chester Harding, Corp. Tech. Elmer G. Harelson, Pvt. William F. Blanchard, and Pfc. Donn F. Schmidel. This quartet presented numerous musical performances to Fort Ord soldiers.

Sports were also a key factor in helping keep soldiers busy and enhancing unit *esprit de corps*. This photograph shows a Fort Ord soldier baseball team during World War II.

Hollywood motion picture studios frequently highlighted their starlets in morale-raising photographs sent to military newspapers. This photograph of Leslie Brooks of Columbia Pictures appeared in the Christmas 1942 issue of the *Fort Ord Panorama* with the inscription, "To the boys at Fort Ord—Merry Xmas, Leslie Brooks."

In 1940, General Stilwell proposed the construction of a "Soldiers' Club" as a recreational facility for enlisted soldiers at Fort Ord. It would be one part of a large entertainment and sports complex for all Fort Ord military personnel. This August 1, 1942 photograph shows the front, or east exterior side of the Soldiers' Club under construction. This building was located on bluffs overlooking the Monterey Bay.

The Fort Ord Soldiers' Club, including a swimming pool in front, was completed in 1943.

This 1943 postcard shows the foyer of the Fort Ord Soldiers' Club.

The Fort Ord Solders' Club is pictured here in the World War II era.

During World War II, Fort Ord soldiers also had the opportunity to rest and relax at the newly constructed U.S.O. (United Service Organization) Club in nearby Salinas.

Elements of the 3rd Amphibian Special Brigade trained at Fort Ord during World War II prior to deploying to the Pacific Theater of Operations. This was one of their recruiting ads. It is unknown how many "boys" were attracted to Fort Ord, on the "coast of sunny California," as a result of this recruiting campaign.

This photograph, taken on February 21, 1942, shows Company E, 58th Quartermaster Battalion, reportedly the largest company at Fort Ord.

In this *c.* 1941 photograph, a building labeled "Transportation Officer" is relocated from the main Fort Ord cantonment area to East Garrison.

These two noncommissioned officers worked in the G-2 (Intelligence) Section of the 7th Infantry Division staff. Working diligently at their desks are Sergeant Shirly (left) and Sergeant Bergman (right) in 1941.

Soldiers of the 1st Medical Regiment, Fort Ord, enjoy the scenic view while participating in a unit march at the nearby spectacular Pinnacles National Monument on April 9, 1942.

Fort Ord soldiers practice hand-to-hand fighting in 1942. From the looks on the faces of many of the soldiers, this training may have been posed and conducted for the photographer.

Military service, especially in wartime or during periods of danger, tends to make people more religious. This photograph depicts Fort Ord soldiers attending Easter services in the North Chapel on April 5, 1942. The U.S. Army built 482 chapels, similar to this one and each designed to hold 400 people, on new military posts in the United States in 1940 and 1941.

These M2 series light tanks provided a mobile punch in this 1st Medical Regiment training demonstration at Fort Ord in June 1942.

These soldiers, the crewmembers of this M2 wheeled combat car, participate in a 1st Medical Regiment training demonstration at Fort Ord, June 1942. The weapon aimed where the leftmost soldier is pointing is the Browning M2 .50 caliber machine gun. A Browning M1917A1 .30 caliber water-cooled machine gun is mounted at the rear of the combat car.

Three
1946–1976
THE COLD WAR AND
THE VIETNAM ERAS

At the end of World War II in 1945, Fort Ord became a demobilization center. The 4th Replacement Training Center assumed the responsibility for operating Fort Ord in 1947. The 4th Infantry Division was reactivated shortly thereafter and trained soldiers until 1950, when it moved to Fort Benning, Georgia and was replaced at Fort Ord by the 6th Division. The 6th Division remained at Fort Ord until 1956, when it was replaced by the 5th Division, which had redeployed from Germany. The 5th Division was inactivated on June 5, 1957, and Fort Ord became the United States Training Center, Infantry. The most easily recognizable symbol from that era was the drill sergeant in his distinctive campaign hat. This photograph shows Sgt. 1st Class Henry I. Foss, Fort Ord Drill Sergeant of the Year for 1972.

Fort Ord's airfield was named Fritzsche Airfield to honor Maj. Gen. Carl F. Fritzsche, Fort Ord Commanding General, who was killed in a tragic aircraft accident at Orinda, California, on September 30, 1960.

Fritzsche Army Airfield was dedicated on March 18, 1961. This photograph was taken during the ceremony when the plaque naming Fritzsche Army Airfield was unveiled.

This photograph was taken during the troop review and aircraft display at the Fritzsche Army Airfield dedication ceremony on March 18, 1961.

This 1961 aerial photograph, taken facing northeast, shows Fritzsche Army Airfield with the Salinas River in the background.

The control tower at Fritzsche Army Airfield was still under construction in early 1961.

This 1966 photograph shows the senior officers at Fort Ord. On the right is Maj. Gen. Robert G. Fergusson, Commanding General of the U.S. Army Training Center, Infantry, and Fort Ord, and his wife. On the left is Maj. Gen. Leland G. Cagwin, Commanding General of the Combat Developments Command Experimentation Center (CDCEC), and his wife. CDCEC was a tenant unit at Fort Ord established in 1956 to oversee testing of new combat equipment.

With the expansion of hostilities in the Republic of Vietnam in 1965, Fort Ord also became a staging area for units deploying to Southeast Asia. The primary mission of the U.S. Army Training Center, Infantry, and Fort Ord remained conducting basic and advanced individual training. Training became oriented towards Vietnamese combat conditions and scenarios. This photograph shows a new group of inductees at Fort Ord in the mid-1960s.

Drill and ceremonies became an important part of basic training, as it taught self-discipline, obedience to commands, subordination of the individual, precision and attention to detail, and respect. These basic trainees are at Fort Ord in the late 1960s. In the mid-1960s to mid-1970s, Fort Ord had four training brigades. The 1st and 3rd Brigades conducted Basic Combat Training. The 2nd Brigade provided Advanced Individual Training (Infantry). The 4th Brigade conducted combat support training courses, such as basic army administration, food service, basic unit supply, automotive mechanic's helper, field communications, light wheel vehicle driver, and radio operator.

Road marches, as conducted at Fort Ord in the 1960s, were an essential component of basic and advanced individual training because they improved the physical conditioning, stamina, and confidence of individual soldiers, as well as unit cohesion, teamwork, and *esprit de corps*.

Seen from a drill sergeant's perspective in this mid-1960s Fort Ord photograph, trainees constantly did push-ups to build up their physical fitness and stamina but also as a corrective measure. Drill sergeants were always available to assist and counsel the trainees.

These Fort Ord trainees execute the uneven bars while running the "circuit drill" course in 1974.

The climbing and successful execution of somewhat dangerous obstacles, as shown in this 1970s photograph, increase soldiers' confidence in their abilities and level of physical fitness.

A Fort Ord trainee climbs the cargo net obstacle at the confidence course in the 1970s.

Basic rifle marksmanship and weapons qualification is an integral component of any military training program. In this September 26, 1969 photograph, trainees from Company A, 3rd Battalion, 3rd Brigade, fire the M-14 rifle for qualification on Range #6 at Fort Ord.

Trainees from Company D, 5th Battalion, 2nd Brigade, fire their weapons on the M-60 machine gun qualification range #26, Fort Ord, on September 26, 1969.

Bayonet training helps instill motivation and audacity into trainees, and it shows them not to be afraid of close combat. The elementary moves of the bayonet fighter are taught to trainees at the Fort Ord bayonet course in this November 3, 1969 photograph.

Pugil stick training, in which soldiers conduct simulated bayonet warfare, also helps instill the "spirit of the bayonet" and aggressiveness into each trainee. This Fort Ord photograph is from the late 1960s.

These Fort Ord soldiers participate in map reading and navigation training in the 1970s.

Many aspects of the war in Vietnam revolved around air mobility. In this photograph, a basic training unit is introduced to the techniques of helicopter evacuation of wounded soldiers in a simulated combat situation on October 31, 1969.

This Fort Ord trainee is taught how to operate and maintain the AN/PRC-77 radio in the late 1960s.

Carefully tightening that last gaff strap, this wary communications trainee isn't taking any chances on his first challenging pole climb. A look at the jagged splinters on the pole are reason enough for extra precautions. One careless misstep or a loose piece of equipment and it's a long, rough, and painful slide to the sand below. This training, pictured here on March 21, 1963, is one segment of Fort Ord's field communications crewman course.

Soldiers in the field wireman's course at Fort Ord conduct pole climbing training on September 19, 1969.

The sergeant (second from right) instructs his trainees at the Food Service School at Fort Ord on September 19, 1969.

Lt. Gen. Stanley R. Larsen, Commanding General, Sixth Army (third from right in soft cap), poses with soldiers of the "All Hawaii" Company, Company C, 4th Battalion, 3rd Brigade, Fort Ord, on August 5, 1969.

HELMET

GLOVES

CROTCH PROTECTOR

In late 1969, Fort Ord infantry training included the "Man versus Man Reaction Course." This free-play and realistic training permitted soldiers individually and in small units to maneuver and fire at each other with BB-type guns. The participating soldiers wore helmets with visors for face and eye protection, crotch protectors, and gloves.

Much of the "Man versus Man Reaction Course" training in 1969 took place in and in the vicinity of a simulated Vietnamese village built at Fort Ord.

This 1969 photograph shows part of the Vietnamese village built at Fort Ord for training purposes. The personnel in "black pajamas" are actually U.S. soldiers role-playing Viet Cong.

This platoon of Fort Ord soldiers is dressed as Viet Cong during training at the Vietnamese village area at Fort Ord in 1969.

Fort Ord training to prepare infantry soldiers for Vietnam combat included a foot bridge booby trap, with disabling punji stakes hidden underneath. This photograph was taken on April 15, 1971.

This April 15, 1971 Fort Ord photograph of realistic Vietnam-oriented training shows a bomb booby trap.

Female soldiers of the Women's Army Corps (WAC) were also trained at Fort Ord in the 1960s and 1970s. This March 1974 photograph shows Drill Sgt. Catherine Robbins (center) of Company D, 4th Battalion, 4th Brigade, at Fort Ord.

Drill Sgt. Catherine Robbins trains her female WAC soldiers at Fort Ord in 1974.

Commissioned officer clergymen of all faiths provided religious services and counseling to Fort Ord soldiers in training. This 1970s photograph shows a military rabbi leading a religious service at Fort Ord.

As training at Fort Ord increased during the Vietnam War, a major construction program began in the late 1960s. A new community center was planned for the site at the intersection of Gigling and then–North-South Roads. This October 21, 1968 photograph shows the new Fort Ord Main Post Exchange (PX) under construction.

This October 21, 1968 photograph shows the skeleton of the new Fort Ord Main PX under construction.

The Fort Ord Main PX was completed on December 18, 1970 at a cost of $882,700. The Main PX continues to be operational.

Pictured here on October 21, 1968, a new U.S. Army Hospital was under construction at Gigling Road and Sixth Avenue at Fort Ord.

The Fort Ord U.S. Army Hospital was completed on October 21, 1971 at a cost of $13,373,000. It was named the Silas B. Hayes Hospital, in honor of Maj. Gen. Silas B. Hayes, Medical Corps, U.S. Army (1902–1964), who had served as surgeon general from 1951 to 1959. This building no longer serves as a hospital.

The construction of a new Fort Ord barracks complex is shown under construction along Gigling Road in this October 21, 1968 photograph.

This new basic combat training barracks was completed at a cost of $10,912,000 on March 18, 1970. This building has been vacant since 1993.

Four
1974–1994
THE VOLUNTEER ARMY
AND LOW-INTENSITY
CONFLICT

This new soldier, seemingly somewhat bewildered, arrives at his first permanent duty station, Fort Ord, c. 1976.

The 7th Infantry Division, under the command of Maj. Gen. (later Lt. Gen.) Robert G. Gard, Jr., was reactivated at Fort Ord in October 1974.

Soldiers of the 7th Infantry Division conduct rifle marksmanship training at the Fort Ord "beach ranges" on September 27, 1979.

General of the Army Omar N. Bradley, the U.S. Army's last five-star general, visited Fort Ord c. 1978.

This 1986 aerial photograph, taken facing west and the Monterey Bay, shows Highway 1 and the Fort Ord Main Gate in the upper left-hand corner. The old Gigling railroad spur appears under the date "03-25-86.".

The Soldiers' Club was renamed Stilwell Hall in honor of Gen. Joseph W. Stilwell in 1966, and this photograph was taken in the late 1970s. Stilwell Hall, a landmark of the World War II citizen Army, was "retired" (demolished) in 2003.

The Fort Ord Commissary remained open throughout the 1970s, 1980s, and 1990s and, as of 2003, was still operating and serving both active duty and retired military personnel.

Two large and modern Child Development Centers were built and opened at Fort Ord in the late 1980s.

This 7th Infantry Division "Lightfighter," wearing his distinctive "rag-top" camouflage helmet cover, prepares to rappel from a helicopter.

These two 7th Infantry Division (Light) soldiers low-crawl under barbed wire on an obstacle course during close combat training.

This obstacle challenges, but does not stop, this Lightfighter.

Field medical operations training is conducted by these Lightfighters.

These 7th Infantry Division (Light) soldiers participate in realistic field medical evacuation training.

Spc. Scott A. Wechsler, Company B, 3rd Battalion, 9th Infantry, 7th Infantry Division (Light), assembles a Bangalore torpedo during demolitions training at Fort Ord.

These 7th Infantry Division (Light) soldiers show the TOW (tube-launched, optically-tracked, wire-guided) anti-tank missile launcher system to curious onlookers during a military exhibition in Monterey.

Wearing their chemical protective over garments and masks, these soldiers conduct range firing at Fort Ord with, on the left, an M-60 machine gun and, on the right, an M-16 rifle.

This 7th Infantry Division (Light) soldier prepares to fire the Squad Automatic Weapon (SAW), M-249 light machine gun, at a firing range.

Training was frequent, demanding, and realistic for 7th Infantry Division (Light) soldiers. In this photograph, Lightfighters offload a C-130 aircraft and begin a training exercise.

These heavily loaded but well-trained and camouflaged Lightfighters conduct patrolling operations in a training exercise.

The 7th Infantry Division (Light) deployed to Panama in December 1989 to participate in Operation Just Cause. It was the first time since the Vietnam War that an entire division had been deployed in combat operations. In this photograph, Spc. Wells performs guard duty.

Vice President Dan Quayle talks with 7th Infantry Division (Light) soldiers upon arriving at Tocumen International Airport in Panama on January 27, 1990. Quayle is talking with, from left to right, Spc. Clark Couch, Spc. Russell Howard, Staff Sgt. Anthony Celeste, and Staff Sgt. Armando Triana, all of 2nd Battalion, 27th Infantry.

A local television reporter broadcasts from outside the Fort Ord Main Gate, *c.* 1990.

Secretary of Defense William J. Perry speaks at the ceremony officially closing Fort Ord, effective September 30, 1994.

Five
POST-1994
FROM SWORDS TO
PLOWSHARES

After the 7th Infantry Division (Light) was inactivated in 1993 and Fort Ord closed in 1994, the "Lightfighter" statue near the main gate was moved to Fort Lewis, Washington. Fort Ord contained over 25,000 acres of land when it closed. Land parcels were given to the adjoining communities of Marina and Seaside, with land also being given to educational, law enforcement, and other entities. The Army retained 795 acres of the former Fort Ord and renamed it the Ord Military Community.

The closure of Fort Ord was an exercise in turning swords into plowshares. Many of the more modern facilities of Fort Ord, centered on the Sixth Avenue area, were transferred to the fledgling California State University-Monterey Bay (CSU-MB). Much of the infrastructure has been transformed into educational facilities. The CSU-MB University Center, shown in this photograph, was the former Fort Ord Pomeroy Recreation Center.

The former headquarters building of the 2nd Brigade, 7th Infantry Division (Light) has been renovated and turned into the CSU-MB Information Technology Center.

Located at the corner of Sixth Avenue and Colonel Durham Road, the former headquarters building of the 1st Brigade, 7th Infantry Division (Light) has been vacant since 1993 and remains unoccupied and boarded up.

The former headquarters building of the 3rd Brigade, 7th Infantry Division (Light), located at the intersection of Inter-Garrison Road and the Eighth Avenue Cut-off, has also been vacant since 1993.

These former Fort Ord barracks on Sixth Avenue have been modernized and are currently being used by CSU-MB for classrooms and administrative offices.

Other Fort Ord barracks, built in the early 1950s and boarded up since 1993, contain lead paint, lead pipes, and asbestos insulation. As it would be too expensive to renovate them, they will eventually be razed.

Thousands of temporary "mobilization buildings" were constructed at Fort Ord at the beginning of World War II. As of 1986, 1,086 mobilization buildings remained, and hundreds still stood in 2003. Plans dictate that these buildings will be destroyed, and the 477-acre main cantonment area of Fort Ord will become a significant mixed-use development called West and North University Villages.

These World War II mobilization building are also on the site of the planned West and North University Villages and will also be demolished. West and North University Villages will contain a major shopping district, restaurants, a hotel, a major business park, an arts district, and up to 1,200 living units. Plans exist for the development of 1,400 homes, with a major arts district, in the East Garrison area, as well as for a retirement community in the former Lower Patton Park Army housing area.

The World War II Fort Ord Post Headquarters Building was later renamed Martinez Hall, after Pvt. Joe P. Martinez, Company K, 32nd Infantry, 7th Infantry Division, who posthumously received the Medal of Honor for gallantry in action in the Aleutian Islands in May 1943. Martinez Hall later served as the Fort Ord Officers' Club, the Post centralized in- and out-processing facility, and in 2003 as a Veterans' Transition Center.

This wall mural on a former reconnaissance unit building depicts a U.S. Army frontier scout scanning the horizon for signs of activity. This scout will continue to maintain his lonely vigil at the former Fort Ord.

When it was determined in the early 1970s that basic training would end at Fort Ord in 1976, former drill sergeants and other soldiers decided to create a memorial to the drill sergeant, an outstanding trainer of men and symbol of leadership. Such a monument would also preserve a significant aspect of Fort Ord's outstanding history. Money was raised, and this statue, now located in the Ord Military Community, was dedicated on September 24, 1974. First Sergeant Willie Smith, U.S. Army (Ret.), a former Fort Ord drill sergeant, observed correctly that, "This statue represents every drill sergeant who served here."